HISTORY MYSTERIES

MONSTERS

Paul Mason

Belitha Press

Produced by
Monkey Puzzle Media Ltd,
Gissing's Farm, Fressingfield,
Suffolk IP21 5SH, UK

First published in Great Britain in
2001 by Belitha Press Limited,
London House, Great Eastern Wharf,
Parkgate Road, London SW11 4NQ

ISBN 1 84138 339 2

British Library Cataloguing in
Publication Data for this book is
available from the British Library.

Printed in Hong Kong / China
10 9 8 7 6 5 4 3 2 1

Acknowledgements
We wish to thank the following
individuals and organizations for
their help and assistance and for
supplying material in their
collections: Art Archive 29 (New
York Public Library/Harper Collins
Publishers); Corbis 1 (Bettmann),
5 right (Bettmann), 5 left (Adam
Wolfitt), 6 bottom (Bettmann), 9
(Bettmann), 23 (Bettmann), 24
(Bettmann), 30 (Academy of Natural
Sciences, Philadelphia); Fortean
Picture Library *front cover* (John
Sibbick/Fortean Times), *back cover –
all*, 2, 7 top, 7 bottom (Richard
Svensson), 8 top, 11 top (Lars
Thomas), 11 bottom, 12 bottom
(Richard Svensson), 13 (René
Dahinden), 14 (William M
Rebsamen), 15 top (AN Shiels), 16
(John Sibbick), 17 top (Tony Healy),
18 top (Tony Healy), 19, 20 (René
Dahinden), 21 top (Cliff Crook),
21 bottom (Christopher L Murphy),
22 top, 25, 26, 31; Kobal Collection
8 bottom; Mary Evans Picture
Library 18 bottom; Popperfoto 27
(Phil Reid); Rex Features 4 (Peter
Brooker), 15 bottom, 17 bottom
(Sipa), 22 bottom (Sipa), 28;
Topham Picturepoint 12 top.
Map by Michael Posen.

▼ This beast is a manticore – it has the
head of a man but the body of a giant
animal. Find out more on page 11.

CONTENTS

LOOK FOR THE MONSTER BOX

Look for the little black monster in boxes like this. Here you will find extra facts, stories and other interesting information about monsters.

MONSTERS, MONSTERS EVERYWHERE!

People have always told stories about monsters, and they have always been afraid of strange and frightening beasts. The very first people must have made up monster stories to try to explain odd noises that they didn't understand.

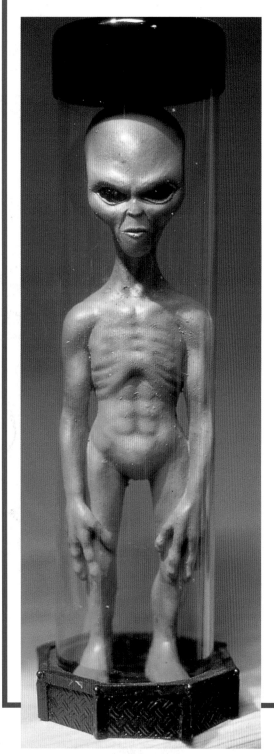

So where do monsters live? Stories about monsters tell of them living in unknown seas, faraway lands and even outer space.

Early explorers told stories of the scary creatures they had met on their travels. Frightened sailors arrived back on land, having been attacked by deep-sea monsters. Stories about vampires, zombies and werewolves were told to frighten children. But there was always a question in the storyteller's mind – could the stories be true?

◄ People claim to have seen monsters both on Earth and in space. This is a model of what an alien monster might look like.

◄ The terrible jaws of a monster can be seen in this stained-glass window.

With most monsters there is always one question for which we don't know the answer. Do they exist or don't they?

► Frankenstein's monster is a very popular story that has been made into a film many times.

FRANKENSTEIN'S MONSTER

In the 1800s Mary Shelley wrote the book *Frankenstein*. The monster in this story became the most famous monster of them all. He was made from different parts of bodies and brought to life by a mad scientist called Frankenstein. The monster had no name.

MONSTERS AROUND THE WORLD

There are said to be monsters all over the world. Some, such as sea serpents, were found in the oceans. Others were only seen in one area. For example, the fur-covered monster Bigfoot has only been seen in parts of North America.

▼ This map shows which monsters are thought to live in which countries.

Zombie

Bigfoot

Yeti

Werewolf

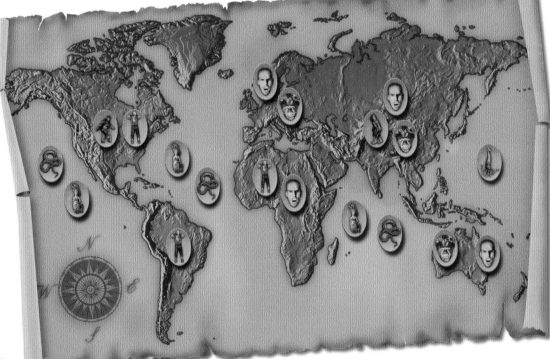

Vampire

Mermaid

Sea Serpent

Giant Squid

◄ A scientist is attacked by the monsters that he brought to life, in the film *Revenge of the Zombies*.

Many monsters only existed in stories. But some were real creatures that were so huge or scary that humans said they must be monsters. For example, although we don't know if sea serpents exist today, we do know that they existed during the age of the dinosaurs. The scariest sea serpent was the *Tylosaurus*, which was 18 metres long with huge jaws. Another real monster that still lives deep in the sea is the oarfish, a huge eel-like sea creature. It is very rarely seen, though scientists believe that they do exist. As they often grow to a length of 12 metres, these huge fish could easily be mistaken for sea monsters.

▲ A colourful Norwegian sea serpent pulls a sailor from the deck of his ship.

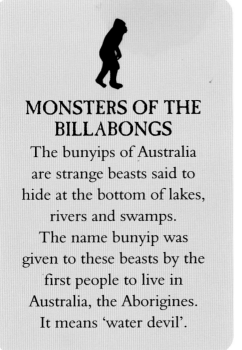

MONSTERS OF THE BILLABONGS

The bunyips of Australia are strange beasts said to hide at the bottom of lakes, rivers and swamps. The name bunyip was given to these beasts by the first people to live in Australia, the Aborigines. It means 'water devil'.

▲ This is an artist's idea of what a bunyip – an Australian monster – looks like.

MONSTERS OF THE SEA

Before humans knew what the rest of the world was like, they thought that monsters were hiding round every corner – especially in far-off seas. Many sailors said they had seen weird and wonderful creatures on their travels.

Many sailors came home with stories about mermaids. These odd-looking sea beasts were half fish, half woman. Perhaps the sailors thought that seals sleeping on faraway rocks were beautiful women with fish-like bodies.

▲ This picture from the 1800s shows a mermaid next to a manatee. The manatee is a real creature that sailors may have mistaken for a mermaid.

Ancient seamen told fantastic stories about another sea creature, the hydra. This was a beast with lots of heads – usually it had nine. If one of its heads got chopped off, two more grew back in its place.

◄ A hero faces the many-headed monster, the hydra, in the film *Jason and the Argonauts*.

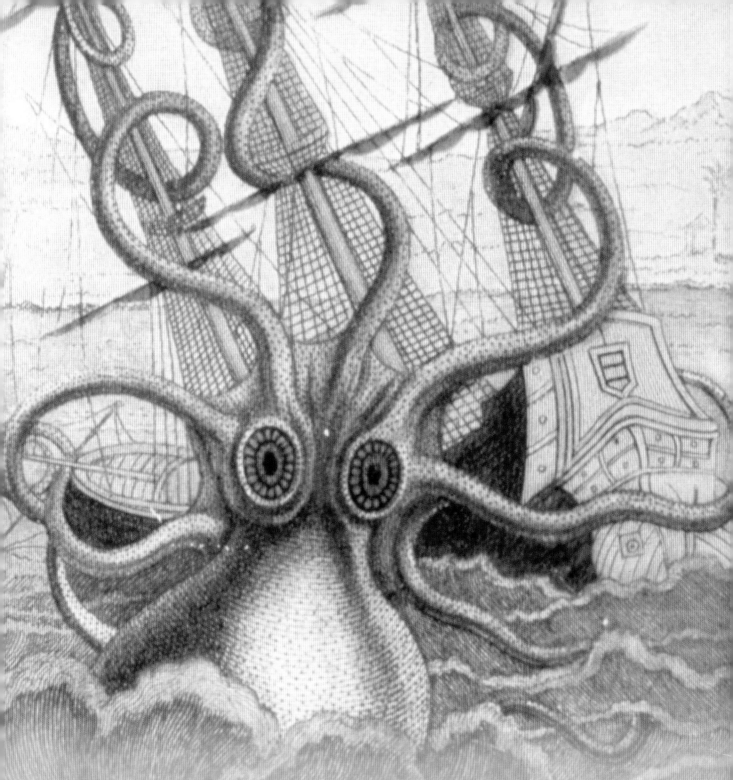

▲ When this picture was painted 200 years ago, people believed that the giant squid could really grow bigger than a ship.

Scary stories of ships being attacked by giant squid may be true. Scientists think a giant squid up to 70 metres long could be hiding at the bottom of the ocean. These huge creatures may have attacked ships thinking that they were whales!

MONSTERS ON THE LAND

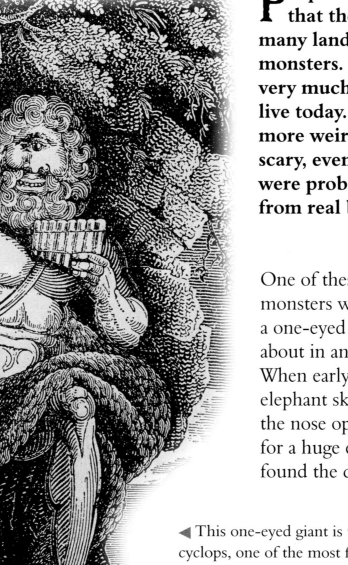

People used to believe that there are just as many land monsters as sea monsters. Some of these are very much like animals that live today. Others are far more weird looking and scary, even though they were probably made up from real beasts.

One of these make-believe monsters was the cyclops – a one-eyed giant first talked about in ancient Greek legends. When early travellers found elephant skulls they thought the nose opening was the hole for a huge eye and they had found the cyclops' skull!

◄ This one-eyed giant is the cyclops, one of the most famous of all legendary monsters.

The gryphon was a wild monster of the skies. Half eagle and half lion, this was a huge creature. Its body was eight times the size of a lion's and its eagle's head and wings were very powerful. The gryphon was said to enjoy the taste of humans.

▲ A gryphon gets ready to swoop down and grab its victim.

People believed that the odd-looking manticore lived in faraway jungles. It had the body of a lion, a man's face and a stinging tail like a scorpion. Its mouth was filled with rows of razor-sharp teeth, and it too was believed to eat any humans that passed its way.

▼ The manticore's tail was said to fire poisonous darts.

MONSTERS OF THE LAKE

Many of the world's big lakes are believed to be the homes of monsters. There are hundreds of lake monsters and more are found every year! The most recent, Kozak, was spotted in 1995 in Lake Van, Turkey.

▼ This hazy picture is said to be of Kozak, the monster from Lake Van in Turkey. It's hard to say what the photograph really shows.

▼ All of the monsters in this drawing are believed to live in Lake Storsjo in Sweden.

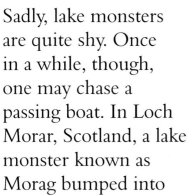

OGOPOGO

Long before Europeans went to live in America, Ogopogo was called *Natiaka* (lake beast) by the Native Americans who lived near Lake Okanagan in Canada. The name Ogopogo comes from a song written in 1926:

'His mother was an earwig,
His father was a whale,
A little bit of head and hardly any tail –
And Ogopogo was his name.'

▲ Ogopogo, the Canadian lake monster, has become so famous that people travel from all over the world to try and catch sight of it.

Sadly, lake monsters are quite shy. Once in a while, though, one may chase a passing boat. In Loch Morar, Scotland, a lake monster known as Morag bumped into a motor boat in 1968. One of the sailors remembered: 'I looked up and a creature was coming directly after us...when it struck the boat it seemed to come to a halt or slow down.' Luckily the boat did not tip over!

Where do these monsters come from? Some people believe that they are the distant relatives of dinosaurs – called plesiosaurs – who were trapped in these deep lakes millions of years ago.

THE LOCH NESS MONSTER

Early in 1934 Arthur Grant was riding his motorbike on the road by Loch Ness, Scotland. As he came round a corner, Grant almost crashed into a strange-looking beast crossing the road.

The creature had a small head, a long neck and a big body with flippers. It was Nessie – the Loch Ness Monster!

▼ This picture shows the time when Arthur Grant was said to have come face-to-face with Nessie.

The first sighting of Nessie was 1,500 years ago when Saint Columba helped a swimmer escape from a monster.

The next sighting of Nessie was in 1933, when people reported seeing an 'enormous animal... rolling and plunging in the loch.' Since then, hundreds of people have tried to prove that she really exists, and thousands claim to have seen the monster. But there is still no real proof that she is there.

▲ This photo of Nessie is one of the most famous ever taken, but some people say that it isn't really Nessie.

▼ This is a model of the Loch Ness Monster. It is based on descriptions given by people who say that they've seen Nessie.

MEET THE MONSTER!

One night out on Loch Ness, Peter Davies saw a huge creature on his sonar machine, which showed him the shapes of things under the water. 'I don't mind telling you it was a strange feeling rowing across that pitch-black water knowing there was a very large animal just 10 metres below. The sheer size of the [creature] was frightening.'

CHUPACABRAS

Stories about chupacabras have been scaring
people for hundreds of years and now some
say they are back again! Chupacabras, sometimes
known as goatsuckers, were last reported
in Central America in September 2000.

At that time, more than 100 sheep
died from unusual bites. The farmers
believed that these wounds showed
that chupacabras had returned.

Chupacabras are said to
be about 1.3 metres tall
with huge red eyes, grey
skin, short clawed fingers
and long powerful legs
like a kangaroo's.
They have a line of sharp
spines or spikes down
their back, and some
people say that they
have wings and can fly.

► This picture of
a chupacabras shows
it sucking the blood
of a goat.

◀ A man holds up a model of the footprint of a chupacabras. The footprint was found near several dead animals.

A chupacabras was shot by a man called Jorge Luis Talavera as it attacked his sheep. People who saw the beast's body said it had long claws and skin as smooth as a bat's, with a crest like a crocodile's running along its spine.

SPACE CREATURES?

Orange balls of light are often seen at the same time as the attacks that chupacabras make on animals. Some people have suggested that chupacabras are actually beasts that have been made by creatures from space.

▶ Balls of fire from outer space, like the one shown in this close-up photograph, are often said to appear at the same time as chupacabras attacks. Are the two things linked?

YETI - THE MOUNTAIN MONSTER

People in the high mountains of the Himalayas have told stories for hundreds of years about a strange, ape-like animal about 2 metres tall. Its name is Yeti (from the Tibetan *yeh-teh*, meaning 'that thing there').

▲ This may be a Yeti skull, although the reddish colour of the hair has led some people to say that it might be from an orang-utan (a big, orange-coloured ape).

◄ This photo of a Yeti footprint was taken by mountain climbers in 1951. It is as long as the axe in the photo, which is at least 30 cm long.

Several mountain climbers have told chilling stories about seeing the Yeti. Tenzing Norgay was one of the first men to climb Mount Everest (the highest mountain in the world). One day when he was in Nepal he met a Yeti. He watched it for several minutes before the Yeti moved off. Later, he and some British mountain climbers followed a Yeti through the snow for 3 kilometres before they lost track of it. All three men were sure that they had been following a Yeti.

◄ This is a drawing of the Yeti, or the 'abominable snowman' as it was also called.

 WHAT IS A YETI?
A Yeti is probably a rare type of large ape that lives in the steamy forests of cut-off valleys. The Yeti that are seen by humans may be lone males, looking for new territory away from the forests.

SASQUATCH

Hiding in the forest areas of the American Northwest is a large but shy creature called Sasquatch.

Sasquatch, meaning 'wild man', is a giant fur-covered beast. It is far larger than a fully-grown human and looks a bit like an ape. The footprints it leaves behind are so huge that some people have called it Bigfoot.

BIG FEET

In 1840 Elkanah Walker, who lived with the Spokane people from the Northwest of America, told how his people thought there were giants who lived on a mountain. The giants hunted and worked at night. Their footprints were said to be half a metre long – sounds like Sasquatch!

▲ This picture of Sasquatch comes from a video that was shot in 1967. Many people think that the film is a fake which was made to trick people into thinking Sasquatch is real.

In England in 1784 there were stories about a 'huge, manlike, hair-covered' creature having been caught in Canada. Ever since, people have been saying that they've seen this beast.

▶ This is a model of a footprint that is over 35 cm long. Nobody is sure yet whether or not this big footprint does actually belong to Bigfoot!

One large white Sasquatch has been seen a few times over the years. It is over 2 metres tall, with a big stomach, blue eyes, a wide pink nose and crooked teeth, and it walks with a limp. The first time it was seen was in the summer of 1988, the last time was in October 1996. It has been seen by a young boy on a fishing trip, two men on a camping trip and a man sawing firewood. None of them know each other, so they can't have got together to make up a such a story!

SASQUATCH MASK

There is a Sasquatch mask at Harvard University's Peabody Museum. It was first worn by the Tsimshian people for special ceremonies. It was made some time around 1850-1870.

◀ This is a close-up view of Sasquatch's head, taken from the video film on page 20.

VAMPIRES

One of the best-known and most-feared of all monsters must be the vampire. Almost every country in the world has some kind of vampire story.

Vampires are people who have died after being bitten by another vampire. They then come back to life as vampires themselves. Vampires live off blood – they especially like human blood. The most powerful vampires can change their shape – becoming a bat, a dog or even a cloud of smoke.

▲ This painting shows what Dracula, the first vampire, may have looked like.

There are plenty of ways to defend yourself against vampires. They are known to hate the smell of garlic and cannot stand the daylight. To fight a vampire and win, it is said that you have to use holy water and crosses because vampires are afraid of anything to do with churches and religion. Vampires can only be killed if a thick piece of wood, called a stake, is pushed through their heart.

▼ Dracula's castle, with its high walls that stopped victims from escaping, may have looked something like this.

THE MOST FAMOUS VAMPIRE

Count Dracula, who was written about in a book by Bram Stoker, is the most famous vampire of all – and some people believe that he was a real person! He was said to live in an old castle in the Carpathian Mountains of Transylvania in Romania. But he then moved to England looking for new victims to bite. Dracula was killed at the end of the novel, but that hasn't stopped him being the star of hundreds of movies.

► The most famous movie vampire of all – Dracula – played by the actor Bela Lugosi.

WEREWOLVES

Stories of werewolves are heard all around the world. Werewolves seem to be human by day but turn into wolves when there is a full moon at night.

The town of Wittlich in Germany was living in fear of a werewolf for years. When the monster was killed the town celebrated by lighting a candle in a specially built room. Many believed that the werewolf would return if the candle ever went out!

► Werewolf stories tell of a man who looks ordinary during the day, but turns into a werewolf under the light of a full moon.

One night in 1988, a group of men were driving past the room when they saw that the candle had gone out. They joked that the werewolf would be back soon. But later that night they heard something attacking a fence. When the men went to find out what was happening they saw a huge, wolf-like creature stand up on its back legs and jump over the fence to get away. Their dog would not follow the beast. The next day, the candle was burning again and the creature hasn't been seen since.

THE WITTLICH WEREWOLF

One of the men who saw the Wittlich Werewolf said, 'The creature we saw was definitely an animal and definitely wolf-like. It was about 2 metres tall, and it jumped a 3-metre security fence after taking three long, leaping steps.'

▼ This picture of a werewolf attacking a man is from 1516 – nearly 500 years ago. Even then, werewolves had been feared for hundreds of years.

MONSTER FACTS

▼ This is a picture of the Jersey Devil, a monster said to come from the Pine Barrens of New Jersey in the USA.

The Skunk Ape of Florida

The Florida Skunk Ape is from the same family as Sasquatch. It gets its name from the horrid smell that warns you it's nearby. Some people say there's no such thing as the Skunk Ape, but plenty of people say they have seen it (and smelt it!).

Sasquatch in Brazil

A relative of Sasquatch has been seen even farther south, in Brazil. *Mapinguary*, the Bigfoot of Brazil, has been described as 'roaring in the blackness of the night'.

Yeti head

In Nepal there is a piece from a dead animal's head, said to be the scalp (the skin that covers the top of the head) of a Yeti.

Crocodile monster

When the British ship H.M.S. *Iberian* was sunk by a German submarine during the First World War, the men on the submarine were amazed at what they saw. A huge sea animal was thrown up by the explosion and stayed on the top of the sea for 15 seconds. It seemed to be a 20-metre-long crocodile.

Monster and submarine wars

Later in the war, the men from a German submarine were taken prisoner when their submarine was floating on the waves. They said that they could not go under the water because their submarine had been damaged in an attack by a huge sea beast!

Giant squid attack

In 1930 a ship, the *Brunswick*, was attacked three times in one day by a giant squid. The squid hit the ship and tried to wrap its many legs around it. The third time, it took hold of the propeller and was chopped up by its sharp edges.

Slimy slim

The prize for the monster with the best name must go to Slimy Slim, a lake monster from Lake Payette in Idaho, USA. Slimy Slim was seen in the lake during the 1930s, and has not been seen since. At exactly the same time, quite a few people said they saw a huge crocodile in the lake. The real Slimy Slim may in fact have been a crafty crocodile!

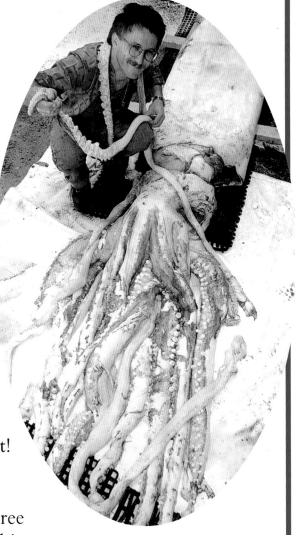

▲ This is a photo of one of the largest ever giant squid, which was over 7 metres long. That's nowhere near as big as the squid on page 9!

MONSTER WORDS

◀ The vampire story is still popular today, in TV shows such as *Buffy the Vampire Slayer*.

ape
An animal, such as a gorilla or orang-utan, with a similar shape to a human.

chupacabras
Also called the goatsucker, chupacabras is a 1.2-metre-tall scary-looking creature that sucks the blood of farm animals and pets.

creatures
Another word for animals.

cyclops
A one-eyed monster in ancient Greek stories that was said to look like a giant.

full moon
The time when the moon is at its biggest and brightest and it is nearly circle-shaped.

gryphon
Half eagle and half lion (but eight times as big), the gryphon was one of the most powerful of all the made-up monsters.

manticore
With a man's face, the manticore also had a lion's body and a stinging tail. Its tail could fire poison darts.

mermaid
Mermaids are said to be half beautiful woman and half fish. They are thought to spend most of their time trying to get sailors to follow them down to the bottom of the sea.

monster
A monster is a make-believe creature – often very big and frightening.

propeller
A blade (knife-shaped object) or set of blades that spin around to push a ship through the water.

Sasquatch
Sasquatch, also called Bigfoot, is a very tall, hairy, human-like creature.

scientists
People who study how things work.

sonar
A way of finding out where things are when they can't be seen easily.

stomach
A general word for the lower part of the body, below the chest.

submarine
A boat that can travel underwater.

werewolves
People who become bloodthirsty wolves when there is a full moon.

Yeti
Yetis are said to live in the Himalayas. They are ape-like and about 2 metres tall.

zombie
A dead person who has come to life again.

▲ The flying fishes in this painting must have seemed very frightening to sailors when they first saw them, but flying fishes are real, they aren't monsters.

MONSTER PROJECTS

Although some monsters are not that different from real animals, most are an odd mixture of bits and pieces from all kinds of beasts. Some of the bits were taken from creatures we know; some of the pieces were just totally made-up.

Why not try creating your own monster? You could draw one, or make a model. There are plenty of beasts in this book to give you some ideas. Remember, monsters are like dinosaurs – no one really knows for sure what colour they are, and no one knows whether your monster will have glowing eyes, green teeth or lots of arms, legs and heads... it's up to you!

▶ The Jenny Hanniver was a very odd-looking sea monster. Some said it had a human head and a body that was a mixture of eagle and manta ray. Others said that it looked like a fish with wings. This is one artist's idea of what it may have looked like.

MONSTER HUNT

Maybe you are lucky enough to have a lake or wood near you where people have seen strange creatures. You could find out more details from your local library or tourist information centre.

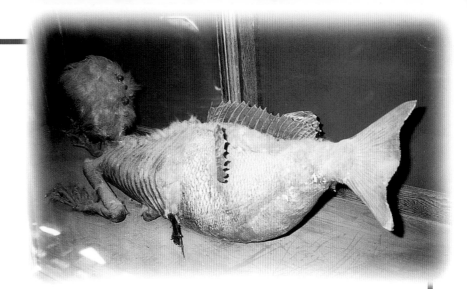

You could also try to think where a monster might live in your area. Perhaps an old building, or a spooky bit of grass. What would he look like? What would he eat? Would he be fierce or very shy and timid? You could write a police report about what the monster looks like, whether it's friendly or not and how to catch it!

▲ This 'mermaid' can be seen in Banff, Canada. It is really made of the end of a stuffed fish and some wood – it isn't a mermaid at all!

MONSTERS ON THE WEB

The best way to find things on the Internet is to type the name of your favourite monster into lots of different search engines. The following are some good sites for monster information:

http://www.paranormalatoz.com – an A to Z of strange things.

http://theshadowlands.net/serpent.htm – information about sea serpents and lake monsters.

http://webhome.idirect.com/~donlong/monsters/monsters.htm – an encyclopedia of monsters.

http://www.draw123.com/ – how to draw monsters.

INDEX